occasionally
appetizers
unforgettable finger foods

by chrisy toombs

ISBN 979-8-9901949-3-9

Every effort has been made to ensure that the recipes contained in this book are
accurate and safe to follow. However, readers are advised to use their judgment
and consider their dietary restrictions and allergies. The author and publisher are
not liable for any damages arising directly or indirectly from the use of the recipes
contained herein.

hello there
i'm chrisy toombs

As the foodie extraordinaire behind HomemadeHooplah.com, I've curated an ever-growing collection of easy, entertaining eats. My passion for crafting deliciously fun foods, ideal for any gathering or potluck, inspired me to share these creations with you—not just on Homemade Hooplah but also through vibrantly delicious cookbooks like this one. You might have even come across my recipes featured on sites like BuzzFeed, Delish, Country Living, and Good Housekeeping.

Originally from Virginia, I now call Phoenix, Arizona, my home, where I live with my boyfriend and our two adorable dogs. Beyond the culinary world, I'm an avid gamer, a lover of good movies, and a devourer of paranormal novels.

Scan the above QR code to visit HomemadeHooplah.com for additional tips, tricks, and guides for all of the recipes in this book.

table of contents

enchilada cups

A fun twist on popular taco cups, enchilada cups are made with a baked tortilla cup filled with savory ground beef, taco seasoning, and red enchilada sauce.

makes: 10 servings   **prep**: 25 mins
cook: 25 mins

ingredients

10 small flour tortillas

1 pound ground beef, 80-85% lean

10 ounces red enchilada sauce

2 tablespoons taco seasoning

14 ounces canned black beans, rinsed and drained

1/2 cup canned corn

1/4 cup chopped pickled jalapenos

1 1/2 cups shredded Mexican blend cheese

1/4 cup chopped fresh cilantro, optional

1 stalk green onion, chopped, optional

1/4 cup chopped tomato, optional

1/4 cup sour cream, optional

1 small avocado, cubed, optional

directions

1 Preheat oven to 350°F.

2 Spray a muffin tin with cooking spray. Insert a tortilla into each cavity to form a bowl. To help tortillas maintain shape while baking, place a tin foil ball in each cup.

3 Bake for 15 minutes or until crispy. Remove muffin tin from oven and discard tin foil balls. Set pan aside.

4 In a large skillet over medium-high heat, add ground beef. Cook and crumble until almost no pink is left, about 8-10 minutes. Drain well.

5 Add enchilada sauce and taco seasoning, then stir until incorporated.

6 Add black beans, corn, and jalapenos, then mix well.

7 Spoon beef mixture into each baked tortilla cup until nearly full. Top each cup with shredded Mexican blend cheese.

8 Bake tortilla cups for 10 minutes or until cheese is melted.

9 Remove muffin tin from oven. Top each enchilada cup with cilantro, green onion, tomato, sour cream, and avocado (all optional).

10 Serve as desired.

ingredients

1.6 ounces buffalo wing seasoning, roughly 3 tablespoons

1 1/2 tablespoons hot sauce

1 1/2 teaspoons garlic powder

1 pound raw medium shrimp, peeled and deveined, patted dry

2 tablespoons olive oil

buffalo shrimp

These sauteed buffalo shrimp combines buffalo seasoning and hot sauce to create a fiery appetizer or dinner.

makes: 4 servings   **prep**: 10 mins
cook: 5 mins

directions

1 In a large bowl, use a spatula to mix together buffalo wing seasoning mix, hot sauce, and garlic powder until combined.

2 Add raw shrimp to bowl and use spatula to toss shrimp, thoroughly coating them with sauce.

3 In a large skillet over medium heat, warm olive oil. Add shrimp to skillet in a single layer and saute for 2 minutes, not moving shrimp. Flip shrimp and cook for 1 minute more or until shrimp are pink, opaque, and curled.

4 Serve as desired.

grape jelly meatballs

Tender meatballs slow cooked in a sweet sauce made with grape jelly and chili sauce. Makes for a fun changeup of traditional cocktail meatballs for parties!

makes: 8 servings   **prep**: 5 mins   **cook**: 2 hours

ingredients

1 1/2 cups grape jelly

12 ounces chili sauce

1 pinch cayenne pepper, (optional)

48 meatballs, frozen, Italian or Swedish style

directions

1   In a medium bowl, whisk together grape jelly, chili sauce, and cayenne pepper. Taste test sauce and adjust cayenne pepper, if needed.

2   Add frozen meatballs to a slow cooker. Pour grape jelly sauce on top and use a spatula toss and coat meatballs.

3   Cover slow cooker and cook on HIGH for 2 hours or LOW for 4 hours.

4   Serve as desired.

ingredients

Buttermilk Cheddar Biscuits

2 cups all-purpose flour, plus more for working dough

1/2 cup unsalted butter, very cold or frozen, cut into tablespoon-sized slices

2 teaspoons baking powder

1 teaspoon granulated sugar

1 teaspoon salt

1/2 teaspoon garlic powder

1/4 teaspoon baking soda

1/4 teaspoon cayenne pepper, optional

1 1/2 cup shredded cheddar cheese

1 cup buttermilk, very cold

Melted Garlic Butter

2 tablespoons unsalted butter

2 teaspoons chopped fresh parsley

1/2 teaspoon garlic salt

cheddar bay biscuits

Bring a restaurant favorite home with this spot-on recipe for Red Lobster's cheddar bay biscuits, baked soft and fluffy and topped with melted garlic butter.

makes: 8 servings   **prep**: 30 mins   **cook**: 12 mins

directions

1 **For the Buttermilk Cheddar Biscuits**

2 Preheat oven to 400°. Line a baking sheet with parchment paper, then set aside.

3 In a food processor, add flour, butter, baking powder, sugar, salt, garlic powder, baking soda, and cayenne pepper. Pulse mixture until butter absorbs dry ingredients and is broken down into small or pea-sized pieces.

4 Next, add cheddar cheese and buttermilk, pulsing again until dough starts to clump together.

5 Remove dough and transfer it to a clean, floured surface. Using your hands, press dough out until 1/2 inch thick, fold in half, and press dough out again to 1/2 thickness. Repeat this folding process two more times, for a total of four folds.

6 For a final time, press dough out until 1/2 inch thick. Dip biscuit cutter in flour, then firmly press cutter down into dough (do not twist) to cut out biscuits. Transfer cut biscuits to prepared baking sheet. Repeat this step until all dough is used (typically 6-8 biscuits).

7 Bake biscuits for 12 to 13 minutes or until biscuits are lightly browned.

8 **For the Melted Garlic Butter**

9 While biscuits bake, prepare garlic butter. In a small bowl, whisk together melted butter, parsley, and garlic salt.

10 **Putting it All Together**

11 When biscuits are fresh from oven, use a pastry brush to generously coat tops of buttermilk cheddar biscuits with melted garlic butter.

12 Allow finished cheddar bay biscuits to cool for 5 minutes.

13 Serve as desired.

bacon wrapped scallops

The ultimate combination of land and sea, these bacon-wrapped scallops serve up crispy bacon and juicy scallops.

makes: 4 servings **prep**: 25 mins
marinate: 1 hour **cook**: 35 mins

ingredients

3 cups milk, or enough to cover scallops in a bowl (optional)

3 tablespoons salted butter, melted and slightly cooled

1 pinch salt

1 pinch black pepper

20 scallops, medium to small with tough muscles removed

10 slices bacon, cut in half

1 teaspoon chopped fresh chives

1 pinch smoked paprika, (optional)

directions

1 **Optional step**: To tenderize scallops and remove any fishy oders, add scallops to a shallow bowl and cover with milk. Set bowl in refrigerator and let soak for 1 hour. Drain, rinse with cool water, and pat scallops dry with a paper towel.

2 Preheat oven to 425°F. Place a 9x13 baking dish nearby. If using wooden skewers, soak them in water for at least 30 minutes.

3 In a medium bowl, add melted butter, salt, and pepper. Add scallops and toss to coat.

4 Take a scallop from melted butter and wrap in a piece of bacon. Thread wrapped scallop onto a skewer, ensuring both ends of bacon are secured. Load up a skewer with around 5 scallops, then rest it across a baking dish so ends of skewer rest on dish edges and scallops are suspended over middle of dish. Repeat this step until all scallops are wrapped, threaded, and positioned over baking dish.

5 Bake bacon-wrapped scallops in oven for 20 minutes. Turn skewers, then bake for another 15 minutes or until bacon is cooked and scallops are opaque

6 Arrange bacon-wrapped scallops on a serving plate and sprinkle with chopped chives and smoked paprika (optional).

7 Serve as desired.

spicy boiled peanuts

Simple and easy spicy boiled peanuts are a salty and flavorful snack with a delicate crunch and a zing of creole spices.

makes: 12 servings   **prep**: 10 mins
cook: 8 hours

directions

1 In a large stockpot, add peanuts, salt, creole seasoning, garlic powder, paprika, and onion powder.

2 Pour in water until peanuts are covered. TIP: press down on peanuts in pot; water should easily cover top layer of peanuts. Depending on size of pot, you may not need all of water listed in recipe. Once done, mix ingredients well.

3 Place stockpot over high heat. Bring to a boil, then reduce to a simmer. Cover and let peanuts simmer for 6-8 hours, stirring every 30 minutes or so. If water level goes down, add more warm water. Over time, peanuts will become saturated with liquid and sink to bottom; this is okay.

4 Drain peanuts from water. Spread out on a baking sheet and allow to dry (optional).

5 Serve as desired.

ingredients

2 pounds in-shell raw peanuts, thoroughly washed

1/4 cup kosher salt

1/4 cup creole seasoning

2 teaspoons garlic powder

2 teaspoons smoked paprika

1 teaspoon onion powder

4 quarts water

cheesy garlic bread

A blend of buttery garlic, a melody of melted cheese, and herbs atop crispy French bread.

makes: 14 servings   **prep**: 25 mins
cook: 15 mins

directions

1 Preheat oven to 400°F. Line a baking sheet with parchment paper, then set aside.

2 In a small bowl, whisk together butter, garlic, garlic powder, thyme, and oregano.

3 Arrange French bread halves on prepared baking sheet with cut sides facing up. Spread garlic butter mixture over cut sides of bread.

4 Bake uncovered for 5 minutes.

5 Remove from oven and top bread with mozzarella, Colby, and Parmesan cheese.

6 Bake uncovered for another 10-15 minutes or until cheese is melted and bubbly.

7 Remove from oven and garnish with fresh parsley. Let rest for 2-5 minutes, then cut into 1-inch sticks (optional).

8 Serve as desired.

ingredients

1/2 cup salted butter, softened

1 1/2 teaspoons minced fresh garlic

1 teaspoon garlic powder

1 teaspoon dried thyme

1 teaspoon dried oregano

1 loaf French bread, sliced horizontally

1 cup shredded mozzarella cheese

1 cup shredded Colby cheese

1/2 cup shredded Parmesan cheese

chopped fresh parsley, for garnish

ingredients

1 pound boudin sausage, precooked or fully cooked

8 ounces cream cheese, softened

8 ounces sour cream

1 cup shredded cheddar cheese

1/4 cup chopped green onion, divided

boudin dip

This Louisiana-inspired boudin dip is baked hot and bubbly with spicy boudin Cajun sausage, a mix of cheeses, and sour cream.

makes: 6 servings   **prep**: 40 mins   **cook**: 30 mins

directions

1 Note: Depending on your region or access, "boudin" or "Cajun" sausage may come raw or pre-cooked. Check package directions to ensure which type you have. If you have cooked sausage, you can move on to next step (there's no need to cook it again first). If you have raw sausage, it should be fully cooked and crumbled before moving forward.

2 Preheat oven to 350°F. Spray a 9x5 baking dish (or similar size - should be able to hold 1 quart) with cooking spray, then set aside.

3 Prepare sausage by removing any casings and crumbling into small pieces (should be 1/2 inch or less in size). Tip: for best results, use your hands to crumble sausage; this way you can feel any remaining pieces of casing or other undesirable parts and remove them. Once crumbled, set sausage aside.

4 Using a stand mixer (or a hand mixer + large bowl), mix cream cheese and sour cream on medium speed until smooth, about 5 to 7 minutes.

5 Add cheddar cheese, 2 tablespoons of green onion, and cooked sausage to bowl, then use a spatula to thoroughly mix all ingredients together.

6 Pour dip mixture into prepared baking dish, spreading out and pressing it into an even layer.

7 Bake dip for 30 minutes or until cheese is melted and bubbly.

8 Garnish dip with remaining 2 tablespoons of green onion.

9 Serve as desired.

ingredients

Baked Chicken Wings

3 pounds chicken wings, prepped for cooking

1 tablespoon baking powder

1 teaspoon fine sea salt

1 pinch black pepper

Teriyaki Sauce

1 1/4 cups water, divided

1/4 cup soy sauce

1/4 cup light brown sugar, packed

2 tablespoons honey

1/2 teaspoon ground ginger

1/4 teaspoon garlic powder

2 tablespoons cornstarch

chopped green onion, for garnish (optional)

sesame seeds, for garnish (optional)

teriyaki chicken wings

These crispy teriyaki chicken wings are baked to perfection and coated in a simple homemade teriyaki sauce. Perfect as a flavorful snack or tasty party food!

makes: 6 servings   **prep**: 35 mins   **cook**: 50 mins

directions

1 For the Chicken Wings

2 Preheat oven to 400°F. Line a baking sheet with parchment paper and place an oven-safe wire baking rack on top. Set baking sheet aside.

3 Pat chicken wings dry with paper towels, then transfer them to a large bowl. Add baking powder, sea salt, and black pepper. Use a spatula or a pair of tongs to toss chicken wings until evenly coated.

4 Bake chicken wings for 40-45 minutes, turning halfway through. Wings are done when skin turns light golden brown and juices run clear.

For the Teriyaki Sauce

5 In a medium saucepan over medium heat, add 1 cup water, soy sauce, brown sugar, honey, ginger, and garlic. Let mixture come to a boil, whisking frequently.

6 While sauce cooks, create a slurry by adding remaining 1/4 cup water and cornstarch to a small bowl, then whisk until cornstarch is dissolved.

7 Pour slurry into saucepan, then bring back to a boil, whisking frequently. Once boiling, cook for 1-2 minutes or until desired thickness is reached. For best results, sauce should easily coat the back of a spoon.

8 Remove teriyaki sauce from heat and let cool slightly, about 5-10 minutes.

Putting it all Together

9 Working quickly, place baked chicken wings in a wide bowl, then pour 3/4 cup prepared teriyaki sauce on top. Use a spatula or a pair of tongs to toss chicken wings until evenly coated.

10 Serve teriyaki chicken wings as desired with remaining teriyaki sauce, chopped green onion, and sesame seeds for garnish (all optional).

candied bacon

This deliciously crispy and sweet baked candied bacon is perfect for a fun twist on breakfast, a new finger food snack, or even as a garnish in a Bloody Mary.

makes: 12 servings   **prep**: 15 mins
cook: 30 mins

directions

1 Preheat oven to 375°F.

2 Whisk light brown sugar, water, and cayenne pepper in a small bowl until sugar dissolves. Set aside.

3 Arrange bacon in a single layer on a rack in a broiler pan. Using a basting brush, generously brush each bacon slice with sugar mixture, reapplying to any dry pieces. Keep applying sugar mixture untill is used.

4 Bake bacon for 25-35 minutes or until crispy, adjusting time for bacon thickness. Check frequently.

5 Transfer bacon to a plate. Cool for at least 5 minutes or cool compeltely to set candied coating.

6 Serve as desired.

ingredients

1/2 cup light brown sugar, packed

2 tablespoons water

1/4 teaspoon cayenne pepper, or to taste

12 slices applewood smoked bacon

bacon ranch stuffed celery

With the crisp crunch of celery topped with a creamy mix of cheese, ranch, and bacon, these stuffed celery sticks are perfect for snacking or feeding a crowd.

makes: 32 servings **prep**: 30 mins **cook**: 15 mins

ingredients

1/2 pound bacon, cooked and crumbled (about 7 slices)

8 ounces cream cheese, softened

1 cup shredded sharp cheddar cheese

1 tablespoon ranch dressing mix

2 stalks green onion, thinly sliced

8 large celery stalks, washed and dried, cut into fourths

directions

1 Using a stand mixer (or hand mixer + medium bowl), mix cream cheese, bacon, sharp cheddar cheese, ranch seasoning mix, and green onion until smooth and creamy, about 2-3 minutes.

2 Using a butter knife, spread bacon ranch filling in natural groove of celery pieces. Repeat this step until all filling is used.

3 Serve as desired.

mississippi sin dip

Straight from a Southern kitchen, this Mississippi sin dip is made with a mix of cheese, tender ham, and fresh green onions, all served in a crispy bread bowl.

makes: 4 servings **prep**: 30 mins
cook: 45 mins

ingredients

1 loaf round bread, such as French or Italian

1 1/2 cups sour cream

6 ounces cream cheese, softened

1 teaspoon Worcestershire sauce

1 pinch black pepper, to taste

1 1/2 cups shredded sharp cheddar cheese

1/4 cup chopped green onion, plus more for garnish

1/2 cup cooked chopped ham, plus more for garnish

directions

1 Preheat oven to 350°F. Set a baking sheet nearby.

2 Carve a hole in top of French bread and remove the soft interior to create a cavity, leaving a thick shell. If desired, save bread for dipping.

3 Using a stand mixer (or a hand mixer + large bowl), whip sour cream and cream cheese until smooth, about 2-4 minutes.

4 Remove bowl from mixer. Add Worcestershire sauce, black pepper, cheddar cheese, green onion, and ham to bowl, then use a spatula to gently fold ingredients together.

5 Place hollowed-out round bread on baking sheet and spoon dip inside. Top with more green onions or ham as desired.

6 Wrap bread in aluminum foil and bake for 30-35 minutes, checking occasionally, until cheese is melted and bread is warm but not too crispy.

7 Transfer Mississippi sin dip to a serving bowl with reserved bread pieces for dipping. Garnish top of dip with more green onion and ham (both optional).

8 Serve as desired.

asian chicken meatballs

With rich flavors of soy, ginger, and garlic, these asian chicken meatballs are a crowd-pleasing finger food.

ingredients

Chicken Meatballs

2 pounds ground chicken

1/2 cup panko breadcrumbs

1/4 cup diced green onion

1 teaspoon ginger paste

1 teaspoon minced fresh garlic

1 teaspoon sesame oil

1 teaspoon garam masala

1/2 teaspoon Szechuan pepper

1 large egg, lightly beaten

Spicy Soy-Ginger Sauce

2 tablespoons light brown sugar, packed

1 cup soy sauce

2 teaspoons sesame oil

2 tablespoons garlic chili paste

1 teaspoon ginger paste

1/2 teaspoon white pepper

2 red chili peppers, whole

1 teaspoon cornstarch

1 teaspoon water

makes: 8 servings   **prep**: 40 mins   **cook**: 20 mins

directions

For the Chicken Meatballs

1 Preheat oven to 400°F. Line a baking sheet with parchment paper, then set aside.

2 In a large bowl, add ground chicken, panko breadcrumbs, diced green onions, ginger paste, garlic, sesame oil, garam masala, Sichuan pepper, and egg. Using a spatula (or even just your hands), mix or knead meat into dry ingredients until thoroughly combined.

3 Scoop out 1-2 tablespoons of meat mixture and work it with your hands. For best results, gently press meat as you roll it into a ball; doing this will help meatballs keep their shape. If there are any seams along meatball surface, pinch them closed, then roll meatball between your hands until smooth. Take about 10-20 seconds for each meatball to ensure they're rolled correctly. Once finished, place meatballs on prepared baking sheet; it's okay if meatballs are placed close together, but ensure they're not touching. Repeat this step until all meat mixture has been used.

4 Bake meatballs for 20 minutes or until cooked through.

For the Spicy Soy-Ginger Sauce

5 While meatballs bake, prepare sauce. In a large saucepan over medium low heat, add brown sugar, soy sauce, sesame oil, garlic chili paste, ginger paste, and white pepper, then whisk well.

6 Add red chili peppers to pan. Heat until sauce begins to simmer and sugar has dissolved, about 5-10 minutes

7 Remove red chili peppers from heat and discard.

8 In a small bowl, whisk together cornstarch and water, creating a slurry. Using same whisk, slowly pour in slurry into saucepan while whisking constantly.

9 Turn off heat but leave saucepan on burner. Cover and let sauce rest and thicken while meatballs finish cooking.

Putting it All Together

10 Remove meatballs from oven. Let rest for two minutes.

11 Transfer meatballs to a large bowl and pour prepared Asian sauce on top. Use a spatula to gently toss and coat.

12 Serve as desired.

strawberry bruschetta

Party-ready bruschetta featuring strawberries, goat cheese, basil, and balsamic, all piled on a baguette slice.

makes: 48 servings   **prep**: 35 mins
cook: 5 mins

directions

1 Preheat oven to 400°F. Line a baking sheet with parchment paper.

2 Arrange sliced baguette pieces on prepared baking sheet, spacing about 1 inch apart. Using a basting brush, coat tops of bread with olive oil and season with salt and pepper.

3 Bake bread for 5 minutes or until edges look golden brown.

4 While bread is still warm, sprinkle (or spread) goat cheese on sliced baguette. Arrange sliced strawberries on top, then sprinkle with basil. Finish by drizzling balsamic glaze on top.

5 Serve as desired.

ingredients

1 24-inch baguette, sliced 1/2-inch thick

1 tablespoon olive oil, or more to taste

1 pinch salt, to taste

1 pinch black pepper, to taste

1 1/2 cups strawberries, stems removed and sliced 1/8-inch thick

1 cup goat cheese, crumbles or spread

1/2 cup chopped fresh basil

1/3 cup balsamic glaze

jalapeno popper dip

With gooey cheeses, spicy jalapenos, and a crunchy panko topping, this jalapeno popper dip a must-make party dip.

makes: 6 servings **prep**: 25 mins
cook: 15 mins

directions

1 Preheat oven to 375°F. Spray an 8x8 baking dish (or similar size) with cooking spray, then set aside.

2 Using a stand mixer (or hand mixer + large bowl), cream together cream cheese, sour cream, mayonnaise, and garlic powder on medium speed until combined, about 3 to 5 minutes.

3 Turn off mixer and add cheddar cheese, Mexican blend cheese, 3/4 cup Parmesan cheese, and diced jalapenos to bowl. Gently fold ingredients together with a spatula.

4 Pour dip into prepared baking dish and smooth top into an even layer, then set aside.

5 In a small bowl, mix together panko breadcrumbs, melted butter, and remaining 1/4 cup of Parmesan cheese until panko is saturated.

6 Sprinkle panko mixture on top of dip, spreading into an even layer.

7 Bake dip for 15-20 minutes or until breadcrumbs turn a golden brown.

8 Serve as desired.

ingredients

8 ounces cream cheese, softened

1/2 cup sour cream

1/2 cup mayonnaise

1 teaspoon garlic powder

1 cup shredded sharp cheddar cheese

1 cup shredded Mexican blend cheese

1 cup shredded Parmesan cheese

4 ounces jarred diced jalapeno peppers, drained, plus more for garnish

1 cup panko breadcrumbs

4 tablespoons salted butter, melted

ingredients

2 tablespoons vegetable oil

2 cups chopped white onion

1/3 cup chopped green onion

1/3 cup chopped red bell pepper

1/3 cup chopped green bell pepper

4 cups bite-sized beef chuck pieces, about 1 1/3 pounds

1/3 cup canned tomato sauce

1/3 cup chopped pitted olives, optional

1 chopped hard boiled egg, optional

1/2 tablespoon dried oregano

1 teaspoon paprika

1 teaspoon ground cumin

1 pinch salt, to taste

1 pinch black pepper, to taste

15 empanada dough sheets

1 egg

1 tablespoon water, plus more sealing empanadas

baked beef empanadas

Perfect as an appetizer or easy dinner, these baked beef empanadas are filled with savory beef chuck, onions, peppers, and a delicious blend of seasonings.

makes: 15 servings   **prep**: 45 mins   **cook**: 45 mins   **cool**: 15 mins

directions

1 Preheat oven to 375°F. Line a baking sheet with parchment paper, then set aside.

2 In a large skillet over low heat, warm vegetable oil. Add white onion, green onion, red bell pepper, and green bell pepper to skillet and cook, stirring frequently, for about 3-5 minutes or until onions are translucent.

3 Add beef chuck to skillet and cook, stirring frequently, for about 5 to 7 minutes or until beef is cooked through.

4 Add tomato sauce to skillet and toss and cook with other ingredients for 1-2 minutes.

5 Remove skillet from heat and let cool slightly, about 10-15 minutes.

6 Add olives, hard boiled egg, oregano, paprika, cumin, salt, and pepper to skillet, then mix well.

7 When ready to assemble empanadas, lay out an empanada dough sheet and spoon prepared filling into center. Lightly wet edges of empanada with water, then fold, using your fingers to press down and seal empanada. For pretty presentation, press a fork around edges of empanada. Place empanada on prepared baking sheet. Repeat this step until all empanadas are assembled.

8 In a small bowl, whisk together egg and water. Use a basting brush to coat tops of prepared empanadas with egg wash.

9 Bake empanadas for 20-25 minutes or until tops of empanadas are golden brown.

10 Serve as desired.

pizza dip

This simple pizza dip with creamy cheeses and spicy pepperoni can be whipped up faster than delivery.

makes: 6 servings   **prep**: 20 mins
cook: 10 mins

ingredients

1 1/2 cups shredded Italian style cheese

1/2 cup shredded mozzarella cheese

8 ounces cream cheese, softened

1 teaspoon Italian seasoning

8 ounces pizza sauce

2 tablespoons chopped green bell pepper, or any pizza topping you'd like

2 tablespoons chopped green onion, or any pizza topping you'd like

5-7 pepperoni slices, or any pizza topping you'd like

directions

1 Preheat oven to 350°F. Spray a 9 inch pie plate with cooking spray, then set aside.

2 In a medium bowl, add Italian-style cheese and mozzarella cheese together, then set aside.

3 Using a stand mixer (or a hand mixer + large bowl), whip together cream cheese and Italian seasoning until smooth, about 3 to 5 minutes.

4 Add cream cheese mixture to prepared pie dish and use a spatula to spread it out into a solid, even layer.

5 Sprinkle about half of cheese mixture on top of cream cheese in an even layer.

6 Pour pizza sauce on top of cheese, using spatula to spread sauce while leaving a 1/2 inch space along side of dish (just like a pizza).

7 Add remaining 1/2 of cheese on top of pizza sauce, again making an even layer.

8 Add toppings of your choice to pizza (recommended: pepperoni, green onion, and green pepper).

9 Bake pizza dip for 10-15 minutes or until cheese is melted.

10 Serve as desired.

bacon wrapped jalapeno poppers

A simple appetizer made with a blend of cheeses and seasonings that's baked in jalapeno halves and wrapped in bacon.

makes: 24 servings   **prep**: 20 mins
cook: 25 mins

directions

1 Preheat oven to 400°F. Spray a baking sheet with cooking spray, then set aside.

2 Using a stand mixer (or hand mixer + medium bowl) whip together cream cheese, cheddar cheese, green onion, garlic powder, and onion powder until ingredients are thoroughly combined.

3 Spoon cream cheese mixture into a sliced jalapeno, being careful not to overfill; filling should be even with rim of jalapeno. Repeat this step until all jalapenos are filled.

4 Wrap a single slice of bacon around each filled jalapeno, securing ends of bacon with a toothpick, then place on prepared baking sheet.

5 Bake jalapeno poppers for 20-25 minutes or until bacon is crispy.

6 Allow poppers to rest 5-10 minutes.

7 Serve as desired.

ingredients

8 ounces cream cheese, softened

1 1/2 cups shredded sharp cheddar cheese

2 stalks green onion, thinly sliced

1/2 teaspoon garlic powder

1/2 teaspoon onion powder

12 large jalapeno peppers, cut lengthwise, seeds and ribs removed

12 slices bacon, cut in half

creamy spinach dip

This crowd-pleasing party dip is a creamy blend of sour cream, cream cheese, spinach, and various cheeses.

makes: 6 servings   **prep**: 20 mins
cook: 10 mins

directions

1 Preheat oven to 350°F. Spray an 8x8 baking dish (or similar size) with cooking spray, then set aside.

2 In a large bowl, blend together sour cream and cream cheese until thick and smooth.

3 Add spinach, Monterey jack cheese, Parmesan cheese, dried minced onion, garlic, salt, black pepper, and red pepper flakes to bowl, then stir until thoroughly combined.

4 Transfer spinach dip to prepared baking dish and smooth it out to an even layer.

5 Bake spinach dip for 10 minutes or until hot and cheese is melted.

6 Serve spinach dip immediately with sliced french bread for dipping.

ingredients

1/2 cup sour cream

8 ounces cream cheese, softened

10 ounces frozen spinach, thawed, rinsed, and drained

1 cup shredded Monterey Jack cheese

1 cup shredded Parmesan cheese

1 tablespoon dried minced onion

1 tablespoon minced fresh garlic

1 pinch salt, to taste

1 pinch black pepper, to taste

1 pinch red pepper flakes, to taste

lemon pepper chicken wings

These lemon pepper chicken wings are freshly fried and coated in melted butter and lemon pepper seasoning.

makes: 6 servings **prep**: 25 mins
cook: 1 hour

ingredients

3 pounds chicken wings, prepped for cooking

4 cups vegetable oil, or enough to fill skillet 2-4 inches deep

1 cup all-purpose flour

1 teaspoon salt

1/4 cup salted butter, melted

1 1/2 teaspoons lemon pepper seasoning

2 tablespoons chopped fresh parsley, for garnish (optional)

lemon wedges, for garnish (optional)

directions

1 Line a large plate or bowl with a few paper towels, then set aside.

2 In a large skillet over medium-high heat, add oil to a depth of 2-3 inches. Use a candy thermometer to ensure oil reaches ideal frying temperature of 350°F. Tip: For an accurate reading, ensure thermometer does not touch bottom of pan.

3 While oil heats, place flour and salt in a large Ziploc bag. Gently shake bag to evenly distribute salt.

4 Pat chicken wings dry with paper towels and place them in Ziploc bag. Seal bag and shake to thoroughly coat chicken in flour mixture.

5 Working in batches of 5-7, drop coated chicken wings in heated oil. Fry for 10-12 minutes, turning halfway through. Wings are done when they turn a deep golden brown. Once cooked, place chicken wings on prepared paper towel-lined plate. Repeat this step until all wings are cooked.

6 In a small bowl, mix together melted butter and lemon pepper seasoning. Use a basting brush to coat both sides of fried chicken wings with buttery lemon pepper.

7 Transfer wings to a serving plate and garnish with chopped fresh parsley (optional).

8 Serve as desired.

cajun bacon wrapped shrimp

These bacon-wrapped shrimp feature tender baked shrimp, crispy bacon, Cajun heat, and green onion garnish.

makes: 15 servings **prep**: 20 mins
cook: 25 mins

ingredients

15 large shrimp, peeled, deveined, and tail on

1 1/2 tablespoons Cajun seasoning

5 pieces applewood smoked bacon

2 tablespoons honey

2 tablespoons olive oil

1 1/2 teaspoons cayenne pepper

1 teaspoon minced fresh garlic

1/2 teaspoon black pepper

3 stalks green onion, chopped, for garnish (optional)

directions

1 Preheat oven to 400°F. Line a baking sheet with aluminum foil, then set aside.

2 In a medium bowl, add shrimp and Cajun seasoning, then toss to coat. Let shrimp marinate for 5 minutes.

3 While shrimp marinates, cut each piece of bacon into 3 equal sections (for 15 total strips).

4 Starting from head of shrimp, wrap 1 bacon strip around each shrimp. Secure end of bacon to shrimp with a toothpick. Repeat this step until all shrimp are wrapped.

5 In a small bowl, whisk honey, olive oil, cayenne pepper, garlic, and black pepper, then divide honey pepper sauce into two separate bowls.

6 Using a basting brush, coat both sides of bacon-wrapped shrimp, then place on prepared baking sheet. Repeat this step until all shrimp are coated. Save second half of honey pepper sauce for after baking.

7 Bake bacon-wrapped shrimp for 20 minutes or until bacon is fully cooked and crispy. If bacon is not fully cooked, allow more cooking time, checking in 2-minute intervals until done.

8 Let rest for 5 minutes. Garnish with chopped green onion (optional).

9 Serve as desired.

goat cheese stuffed mini peppers

Tender sweet mini peppers filled with the pleasantly fresh (yet lightly tangy!) flavor of goat cheese and drizzled with balsamic reduction.

makes: 8 servings   **prep:** 30 mins
cook: 5 mins

directions

1 Preheat oven to 400°F. Line a baking sheet with parchment paper, then set aside.

2 Cut each pepper in half and remove ribs and seeds. Arrange cut peppers on prepared baking sheet.

3 Bake peppers for 5 minutes or until slightly tender. Remove peppers from oven and let cool until easy to handle.

4 Use a spoon to fill each cooled pepper half with goat cheese. Avoid overfilling and keep rims of peppers clean.

5 Drizzle balsamic reduction over stuffed mini peppers.

6 Serve as desired.

mango salsa

This mango salsa is a zesty mix of mango, red pepper, onion, cilantro, lime juice, and a delightful kick of jalapeno.

makes: 8 servings   **prep**: 25 mins
marinate: 2 hours

ingredients

1 1/2 cups fresh diced mango, (about 3 mangoes)

1 cup chopped red bell pepper

1/2 cup chopped red onion

1/4 cup chopped fresh cilantro

1/4 cup lime juice

1 medium jalapeno pepper, chopped, seeds and ribs removed

directions

1 In a large bowl, add mango, red bell pepper, red onion, cilantro, lime juice, and jalapeno pepper. Use a spatula to gently mix until all ingredients are evenly distributed and coated with lime juice.

2 Cover bowl and let mango salsa marinate in refrigerator for at least 20 minutes or ideally 2 hours.

3 Serve as desired.

fried pickles

Fried to crispy perfection and with a can't-have-just-one flavor, these fried pickles are a customizable 7-ingredient snack that are perfect for dipping.

makes: 4 servings   **prep**: 20 mins
cook: 30 mins

ingredients

2 cups drained sliced pickles, hamburger dill chips variety

2 quarts peanut oil

1/2 cup all-purpose flour

2 tablespoons yellow cornmeal

3/4 teaspoon creole seasoning

1/2 cup water

1 tablespoon reserved pickle juice

directions

1 Prepare pickles by arranging them in a single layer on a large plate lined with paper towels. Press out as much liquid from pickles as you can with more paper towels to ensure they are as dry as possible so breading can adhere properly. Once done, set pickles aside.

2 Add peanut oil in a wide, deep skillet. Oil should come up at least 3 inches along side of pan. Heat oil to 350°F (using a candy thermometer helps!) Line a large plate with more paper towels and set nearby.

3 While oil heats, add flour, cornmeal, and creole seasoning to a medium bowl, then mix well.

4 Add water and pickle juice to bowl, then whisk until batter ingredients are incorporated.

5 Add dried pickles to batter, then toss to coat. Ensure that pickles are not sticking together and are completely coated, front and back.

6 Carefully drop coated pickles into hot oil, one at a time. If needed, use a pair of tongs or a long skewer to ensure pickles stay separated and are not sticking to bottom of pan. Fry pickles until crispy and light golden brown, about 4 minutes. Transfer fried pickles to prepared paper-towel-lined plate. Repeat this step until all pickles are fried.

7 Serve as desired.

meatball stuffed mushrooms

These party-friendly meatball stuffed mushrooms have a classic homemade meatball nestled in a baby bella mushroom and then topped with marinara and mozzarella.

makes: 28 servings   **prep**: 30 mins
cook: 25 mins

ingredients

1/4 cup Italian breadcrumbs

1 teaspoon garlic powder

1 teaspoon onion powder

1/4 teaspoon fine sea salt

1/4 teaspoon black pepper

1 pound lean ground beef

1/2 cup grated Parmesan cheese, plus more for garnish (optional)

1 large egg

1 pound baby bella mushrooms, cleaned with stems removed

1 1/2 cup marinara sauce, plus more for garnish (optional)

1 cup shredded mozzarella cheese

1 cup chopped fresh basil, for garnish (optional)

directions

1 Preheat oven to 350°F. Line a baking sheet with aluminum foil, then set aside.

2 In a large bowl, whisk together Italian breadcrumbs, garlic powder, onion powder, salt, and black pepper.

3 Add ground beef, Parmesan, and egg to bowl, then use your hands to mix meat into dry ingredients until thoroughly combined.

4 Place a baby bella mushroom on prepared baking sheet, bottom side up. Take 1 tablespoon of meat mixture, roll it into a ball, and place it on top of mushroom. Drizzle about 1-3 teaspoons of marinara sauce on top of each meatball. Repeat this step until all meatball stuffed mushrooms have been formed.

5 Bake stuffed mushrooms for 15-20 minutes or until internal temperature reaches 160°F.

6 Remove stuffed mushrooms from oven. Sprinkle tops with mozzarella cheese, then return to oven. Bake for an additional 5 minutes or until cheese has melted. To brown cheese, turn oven to broil and allow to cook for 1-2 minutes, watching closely.

7 Transfer to a serving plate. Garnish with more Parmesan cheese, marinara, and fresh basil (all optional.)

8 Serve as desired.

ingredients

2 cups sour cream

2 cups mayonnaise

12 slices bacon, cooked and crumbled

1 cup chopped tomato, plus more for garnish (optional)

1 cup shredded cheddar cheese, optional

1 cup shredded lettuce

romaine lettuce leaves, for lining bowl (optional)

2 tablespoons chopped green onion, for garnish (optional)

toasted bread, for dipping

blt dip

The classic sandwich gets the appetizer treatment with this creamy BLT dip. Made with a creamy base, bacon, lettuce, tomato, and served with crispy bread.

makes: 10 servings   **prep**: 20 mins

directions

1 In a large bowl, add sour cream, mayonnaise, bacon, tomato, cheddar cheese, and lettuce. Use a spatula to thoroughly mix all ingredients together.

2 Prepare serving bowl by lining it with whole lettuce leaves (optional) then transfer dip to bowl. Garnish top with green onion and more tomato (both optional).

3 Transfer dip to a serving bowl and provide toasted bread for dipping.

4 Serve as desired.

guacamole

The classic party dip with a mix of creamy avocado, tangy lime juice, spicy jalapeno, fresh vegetables, and spices.

makes: 6 servings   **prep**: 20 mins

directions

1 In a large bowl, add avocado and lime juice and mash together with a fork or a spoon. If desired, you can leave a few bite-sized pieces of avocados whole.

2 Add tomato, jalapeno, yellow onion, cilantro, garlic, salt, and cumin to bowl. Use a spatula to gently fold ingredients together until combined.

3 Serve as desired.

ingredients

4 medium avocados, halved, seeded, and scooped

1 tablespoon lime juice

1 large tomato, chopped, seeds removed

1 medium jalapeno pepper, chopped, seeds and ribs removed (optional)

1/4 cup chopped yellow onion

1/4 cup chopped fresh cilantro

1 1/2 teaspoons minced fresh garlic, or to taste

1 teaspoon salt, or to taste

1/2 teaspoon ground cumin, (optional)

pineapple cheese ball

This retro party dip is full of sweet and savory flavors like green onion, pineapple, red bell pepper, seasoned cream cheese, and chopped pecans.

makes: 10 servings   **prep**: 25
chill: 2 hours

ingredients

16 ounces cream cheese, softened

8 ounces crushed pineapple, thoroughly drained

1/2 cup chopped red bell pepper

1/2 cup chopped green onion

1 teaspoon seasoned salt

1 1/2 cups chopped pecans

directions

1   Using a stand mixer (or a hand mixer + large bowl), mix cream cheese on medium-high speed until smooth, about 2-4 minutes.

2   Remove bowl from mixer. Add pineapple, red bell pepper, green onion, and seasoned salt to bowl. Use a spatula to gently fold ingredients together.

3   Lay out a piece of plastic wrap on a flat surface, then scoop cheese ball mixture into center. Pull up sides of plastic wrap to cover cheese mixture, confining it to middle. Once completely wrapped in plastic, use your hands to smooth cheese into a ball shape. If needed, use a second piece of plastic wrap to secure ends.

4   Transfer wrapped cheese ball to refrigerator and chill until firm, at least 2-3 hours.

5   When ready to serve, spread out chopped pecans on a flat surface. Roll cheese ball in pecans, using your fingers to press and stick pecans to surface.

6   Serve as desired.

baked taco dip

This delicious baked taco dip comes together with a flavorful blend of savory beef, creamy beans, melted cheeses, and zesty spices.

makes: 8 servings **prep**: 20
cook: 18 mins

ingredients

1 tablespoon olive oil

1 pound ground beef

15 ounces refried beans

15 ounces canned black beans, drained and rinsed

1 cup sour cream

2 teaspoons lime juice

1 ounce taco seasoning, roughly 3 tablespoons

1 cup shredded cheddar cheese

1 cup shredded Monterey Jack cheese

1/2 cup chopped Roma tomato

1/4 cup chopped red onion

1/4 cup sliced black olives

1 jalapeno pepper, sliced (optional)

directions

1 Preheat oven to 350°F.

2 In an oven-safe 10-inch skillet over medium heat, warm olive oil. Add ground beef to skillet and cook and crumble until browned, about 5-8 minutes. If necessary, drain any excess grease from pan.

3 Remove saucepan from heat. Add refried beans, black beans, sour cream, lime juice, and taco seasoning to skillet, then mix well. Use a spatula or back of a spoon to spread mixture into an even layer.

4 Sprinkle cheddar and Monterey Jack cheese evenly over ground beef mixture.

5 Cover skillet with aluminum foil and bake for 10 minutes.

6 Remove foil and bake for 8 more minutes or until cheese has melted.

7 Remove skillet from oven. Top dip with Roma tomato, red onion, olives, and jalapenos (optional).

8 Serve as desired.

smoked salmon dip

Smooth and creamy smoked salmon dip has all the flavor of smoked salmon with hints of lemon, dill, and capers. Great to spread on bagels or dip with crackers.

makes: 8 servings   **prep**: 30 mins
chilling: 30 mins

directions

1 In a food processor, add cream cheese, sour cream, mayonnaise, capers, lemon juice, and Worcestershire sauce. Pulse or blend until cream cheese has broken down, about 3 to 5 minutes.

2 Turn off processor and add salmon, dill, green onion, and salt and pepper to taste. Pulse or blend again until salmon is thoroughly chopped and mixture has a smooth texture, about 5 to 7 minutes. Taste test dip; season with more salt and pepper, if necessary.

3 Transfer dip to a bowl and garnish with more fresh dill (optional).

4 Serve as desired.

ingredients

8 ounces cream cheese, softened

1/4 cup sour cream

1/4 cup mayonnaise

2 tablespoons capers, drained

1 tablespoon lemon juice

1/4 teaspoon Worcestershire sauce

4 ounces smoked salmon

2 tablespoons minced fresh dill, plus more for garnish

2 tablespoons chopped green onion

1 pinch salt, to taste

1 pinch black pepper, to taste

corn dip

A Mexican-style corn dip that has an addictively good mix of corn, sour cream, mayonnaise, and cheese that you can throw together in just 15 minutes or less.

makes: 8 servings   **prep**: 5 mins

ingredients

15 ounces corn, any color (white, yellow, etc), drained

22 ounces southwest corn, or Mexican corn, drained

1 cup sour cream

1 cup mayonnaise

1 bundle green onion, chopped, to taste (roughly 1/2 to 1 cup)

2 cups shredded cheese, any flavor

directions

1   In a large bowl, mix together corn, mexicorn, sour cream, mayonnaise, green onions, and cheese. If desired, reserve a few tablespoons of chopped green onion or cheese to garnish top of dip.

2   Serve as desired.

ingredients

1 cup sake

1/2 tablespoon sesame oil

1 1/2 tablespoons minced fresh garlic, divided

1 teaspoon ginger paste

2 pounds chicken wings, prepped for cooking

2 tablespoons salted butter

1 red chili pepper, sliced

1 jalapeno pepper, sliced

1 shallot, sliced

1/2 tablespoon Szechuan peppercorn medley, divided

2 teaspoons flaky sea salt, divided

1 teaspoon rice vinegar

salt and pepper chicken wings

Ultra delicious with Asian-inspired flavor, these salt and pepper chicken wings are baked crispy and tossed with sauteed hot peppers, shallot, and seasonings.

makes: 4 servings   **prep**: 25 mins   **marinate**: 1 hour   **cook**: 20 mins

directions

1 In a large bowl, whisk together sake, sesame oil, 1 teaspoon garlic, and ginger paste until combined.

2 Pat chicken wings dry with paper towels, then add them to bowl. Toss wings to coat with sake mixture.

3 Cover bowl with plastic wrap and let chicken wings marinate in refrigerator for 1 hour.

4 When ready to cook, line a baking sheet with aluminum foil and place an oven-safe baking rack on top. Arrange chicken wings on rack, spacing them so they do not touch. Discard any remaining marinade. Once done, set pan aside.

5 Heat a small skillet over medium heat and preheat oven to BROIL for 10 minutes with a rack 10 inches from broiler.

6 Once skillet is hot, melt butter. Add red chili pepper, jalapeno, shallot, remaining 3 teaspoons garlic, 1-2 teaspoons Szechuan peppercorn medley (to taste), 1 teaspoon salt, and rice vinegar. Stir and saute for 5 minutes. Once done, remove skillet from heat. Taste test sauce and season with remaining Szechuan peppercorn medley or salt, if desired.

7 Bake chicken wings on prepared rack for 8 minutes. Flip chicken wings, then cook for 7 minutes more.

8 Working quickly, place baked chicken wings in a wide bowl, then pour prepared sauteed vegetables and sauce on top. Use a spatula or a pair of tongs to toss chicken wings until evenly coated.

9 Serve as desired.

jalapeno popper puffs

With a fusion of zesty creamy filling and flaky crust, this finger food brings a fiery kick to any gathering or event.

makes: 32 servings   **prep**: 20 mins
cook: 13 mins

ingredients

1 cup bacon, cooked and crumbled (roughly 1/2 pound)

8 ounces cream cheese, softened

1 cup shredded sharp cheddar cheese

1 jalapeno pepper, chopped, seeds and ribs removed

1 stalk green onion, thinly sliced

16 ounces crescent roll dough

directions

1 Preheat oven to 375°F. Line two baking sheets with parchment paper, then set aside.

2 Using a stand mixer (or hand mixer + large bowl), add bacon, cream cheese, sharp cheddar cheese, jalapeno, and green onion. Whip until combined, about 1-3 minutes. Set bowl aside.

3 Unroll crescent roll dough and cut each triangle into 3 long triangles.

4 Place 1 1/2 teaspoons of mixed filling near the bottom, wider part of crescent dough triangle. Roll dough around filling in a crescent shape, then place rolled dough on prepared baking sheet. Repeat this step until all jalapeno popper puffs are formed, placing them roughly one to two inches apart.

5 Bake for 11-13 minutes or until golden brown.

6 Allow jalapeno popper puffs to cool for 5 minutes.

7 Serve as desired.

ingredients

2 medium eggplants, roughly 1.5lb

4 tablespoons olive oil, plus more for brushing eggplants and garnish (optional)

2 tablespoons tahini paste

2 tablespoons lemon juice

1/2 teaspoon minced fresh garlic

1 pinch salt, to taste, plus more for preparation (optional)

1 pinch black pepper, to taste

chopped fresh parsley, for garnish (optional)

pomegranate seeds, for garnish (optional)

baba ganoush

With a delicious smoky and creamy flavor, this savory baba ganoush is perfect as a dip with veggies, a spread for toasted bread, or a garnish for grilled meats.

makes: 8 servings   **prep**: 20 mins   **cook**: 40 mins   **chilling**: 1 hour

directions

1 Preheat oven to 420°F. Line a baking sheet with aluminum foil, then set aside.

2 Prepare eggplants by slicing them in half lengthwise and cutting a few slits in flesh. If desired, sprinkle flesh of eggplant with salt and let it sit for 2 to 3 minutes to "sweat out" any bitterness, then dab dry.

3 Brush insides of halved eggplants with olive oil, then place them on prepared baking sheet, flesh side down.

4 Bake for 30 to 45 minutes or until eggplant skin blackens and starts to wrinkle. NOTE: Prick eggplant with a toothpick; there shouldn't be any resistance. Flesh of eggplant should be very soft and skin easy to remove.

5 Let eggplant cool until easy to touch, about 10 to 15 minutes.

6 In a food processor, add olive oil, tahini, lemon juice, and garlic. Season with salt and pepper, to taste. Mix until combined, about 2 to 3 minutes.

7 Scoop out flesh of cooked eggplants with a spoon, then add it to food processor. Mix again until slightly blended (avoid overmixing) or desired consistency is reached, about 1 to 2 minutes.

8 Transfer prepared baba ganoush to a serving bowl. Cover and chill in refrigerator for one hour. If pressed for time, chill for a minimum of 15 minutes.

9 Garnish baba ganoush with olive oil drizzle, chopped fresh parsley, and pomegranate seeds for garnish (all optional).

10 Serve as desired.

dill dip

This easy dip goes great with chips, veggies, or bread and can be thrown together in flash. Great for holidays, sports parties, or a movie night!

makes: 8 servings   **prep**: 5 mins

ingredients

1 1/2 cups sour cream

1/2 cup mayonnaise

2 tablespoons dried minced onion

1 teaspoon dried dill weed, plus more for garnish (optional)

1 teaspoon dried parsley

1 teaspoon accent seasoning

directions

1 In a large bowl, add sour cream, mayonnaise, dried minced onion, dried dill weed, dried parsley, and accent seasoning. Stir together until thoroughly mixed and smooth.

2 Transfer dill dip to a serving bowl and garnish with more dried dill weed (optional).

3 Serve as desired.

buffalo chicken dip

This deliciously spicy dip is made with wing sauce, shredded chicken, ranch dressing, and various cheeses.

makes: 6 servings   **prep**: 15 mins
cook: 15 mins

directions

1 Preheat oven to 350°F. Spray an 8x8 baking dish (or similar size) with cooking spray, then set aside.

2 In a large bowl, add cream cheese, chicken, Colby Jack cheese, ranch dressing, buffalo wing sauce, cheddar cheese, and salt and pepper (to taste). Use a spatula to thoroughly mix all ingredients together.

3 Scoop dip into prepared baking dish and smooth out top.

4 Bake dip for 15-20 minutes or until dip is warm and cheese has melted.

5 Serve as desired with celery or other veggies for dipping.

ingredients

8 ounces cream cheese, softened

1 cup shredded cooked chicken

1 cup shredded Colby Jack cheese

1/2 cup ranch dressing

1/2 cup buffalo wing sauce

1/2 cup shredded cheddar cheese

1 pinch salt, to taste

1 pinch black pepper, to taste

celery, for dipping

ingredients

1/2 cup olive oil

2 tablespoons lime juice

2 tablespoons white wine vinegar

1 tablespoon honey

1 teaspoon chili powder

1 pinch salt, to taste

1 pinch black pepper, to taste

15 ounces canned black beans, rinsed and drained

15 ounces canned black eyed peas, rinsed and drained

1 cup sweet corn, fresh, thawed, or rinsed and drained

1 cup chopped Roma tomatoes

1 cup chopped fresh cilantro

1 medium avocado, chopped

1/2 cup chopped green bell pepper

1/2 cup chopped red bell pepper

1/2 cup chopped red onion

1 jalapeno pepper, seeded and chopped

cowboy caviar

Loaded with fresh veggies and topped with a tasty vinaigrette, this colorful cowboy caviar is the summer salsa that packs some heat!

makes: 12 servings   **prep**: 30 mins

directions

1 In a small bowl, whisk together olive oil, lime juice, white wine vinegar, honey, chili powder, and salt and pepper to taste until dressing is a smoky red color. Set dressing aside.

2 In a large bowl (I used a 13-quart mixing bowl), add the black beans, black eyed peas, sweet corn, Roma tomatoes, cilantro, avocado, green bell pepper, red bell pepper, red onion, and jalapeno. Pour the prepared dressing in the bowl, then use a spatula to gently mix ingredients and coat with dressing.

3 Serve as desired.

deviled eggs

A go-to finger food for parties, these deviled eggs have the classic mustard-mayonnaise flavor that's easy to customize with other fillings to your liking.

makes: 16 servings **prep**: 50 mins
cook: 10 mins **chill**: 2 hours

ingredients

8 large eggs

2 1/2 tablespoons mayonnaise

1 tablespoon mustard

1 tablespoon dried minced onion, optional

1 teaspoon celery seed, optional

1 pinch salt, to taste

1/2 teaspoon smoked paprika, or to taste, for garnish (optional)

1 tablespoon chopped fresh parsley, for garnish (optional)

directions

1 Place eggs in a medium saucepan, cover with cold water by an inch, and bring to a boil. Remove from heat, cover, and let sit 10-12 minutes. Drain, rinse with cold water, and cool in iced water for 15-30 minutes. Once cooled, peel eggs.

2 Prepare eggs by slicing them lengthwise down center. Scoop out yolks and transfer them to a medium bowl. Use a fork to break apart and fluff yolks. If desired, rinse egg white halves to remove any yolk residue. Arrange egg white halves on a baking sheet or deviled egg tray, then set aside.

3 In bowl with egg yolks, add mayonnaise, mustard, celery seed and dried onion (both optional), and salt. Use a fork to mash all ingredients together until thoroughly combined. Do a quick taste test to make sure mustard, mayonnaise, and salt flavor ratio is to your liking.

4 Transfer mixture to a pastry bag with a decorative tip (or Ziploc bag with corner cut) and gently fill each egg white half with about 1-2 tablespoons of egg mixture.

5 Garnish deviled eggs with smoked paprika and chopped parsley (both optional).

6 Cover prepared deviled eggs and refrigerate for at least 2 hours.

7 Serve as desired.

7 layer dip

With tasty layers of refried beans, sour cream, lettuce, cheese, guacamole, tomatoes, and black olives, nothing beats the presentation and utility of this dip!

makes: 12 servings   **prep**: 20 mins

ingredients

3 cups sour cream

2 ounces taco seasoning, about 2 packages or 4 tablespoons

3 cups refried beans

3 cups shredded lettuce

3 cups shredded Mexican blend cheese

3 cups guacamole

1 cup chopped tomato

1/2 cup sliced black olives

directions

1 In a small bowl, mix together sour cream and taco seasoning mix. Set nearby.

2 In a clear, tall serving bowl able to hold 9 cups, create even layers of ingredients in this order: refried beans, sour cream mixture, lettuce, shredded cheese, guacamole, tomatoes, and olives.

3 Serve as desired.

million dollar dip

Ready in just 5 minutes, this iconic dip combines creamy mayonnaise, cheddar, bacon, almonds, and spices, making it perfect for any party occasion.

makes: 6 servings   **prep**: 5 mins

ingredients

1 1/2 cups mayonnaise

1 cup shredded cheddar cheese

1/2 cup pre-cooked bacon bits

1/2 cup slivered almonds

4 stalks green onion, chopped small

1 teaspoon minced fresh garlic

directions

1 In a large bowl, add mayonnaise, cheddar cheese, bacon bits, slivered almonds, green onion, and garlic. Use a spatula to thoroughly mix all ingredients together.

2 Serve as desired.

buffalo chicken wings

Perfect for a party, these restaurant-style wings are baked to crispy perfection (no deep frying!) and then coated in spicy buffalo sauce.

makes: 6 servings **prep**: 15 mins
cook: 40 mins

ingredients

3 pounds chicken wings, prepped for cooking

1 tablespoon baking powder

1 teaspoon fine sea salt

1 pinch black pepper, to taste

3/4 cup buffalo wing sauce

celery sticks, for serving (optional)

blue cheese dressing, for dipping (optional)

directions

1 Preheat oven to 400°F. Line a baking sheet with parchment paper and place an oven-safe wire baking rack inside. Set baking sheet aside.

2 Pat chicken wings dry with paper towels, then transfer them to a large bowl.

3 Add baking powder, sea salt, and black pepper to bowl, then toss chicken wings to coat.

4 Arrange chicken wings on prepared baking rack, spacing them so they do not touch.

5 Bake chicken wings for 40-45 minutes, turning halfway through. Wings are done when skin turns light golden brown and juices run clear.

6 Working quickly, place baked chicken wings in a wide bowl, then pour buffalo wing sauce on top. Use a spatula or a pair of tongs to toss chicken wings until evenly coated.

7 Serve as desired with blue cheese dressing and celery sticks (both optional).

chipped beef dip

This Yooper classic is a savory dip made from sour cream, mayonnaise, seasonings, and chipped beef folded within. Delicious with bagels or toasted bread.

makes: 12 servings   **prep**: 10 mins

directions

1 In a large bowl, combine sour cream, mayonnaise, chipped beef, accent seasoning, dill weed, garlic powder, and onion powder. Use a spatula to thoroughly mix everything together. If desired, hold out about 1 tablespoon of chipped beef for decorating top of dip.

2 Transfer dip to a bowl and garnish with reserved chopped beef and more dill weed (both optional).

3 Serve as desired with bagel pieces for dipping.

ingredients

2 cups sour cream

2 cups mayonnaise

6 ounces chipped beef, (1 pkg) roughly chopped

1 1/2 teaspoons accent seasoning

1 teaspoon dried dill weed, plus more for garnish (optional)

1/2 teaspoon garlic powder

1/2 teaspoon onion powder

6 bagels, cut into pieces for dipping

pigs in a blanket

Wrapped in crescent roll dough and baked to perfection, they're a classic party food that everyone will love.

makes: 24 servings   **prep**: 35 mins
cook: 12 mins

directions

1 Preheat oven to 375°F. Line a baking sheet with parchment paper, then set aside.

2 Unroll crescent roll dough and cut each triangle into 3 long triangles.

3 Pat Lit'l Smokies dry with paper towels. Place a Lit'l Smokies on a triangle of dough and wrap it up into a crescent shape, then place on prepared baking sheet. Repeat this step until all Lit'l Smokies are wrapped, spacing each one roughly one or two inches apart.

4 In a small bowl, stir together butter, dried minced onion, dijon mustard, poppy seeds, sesame seeds, Worcestershire sauce, and garlic powder.

5 Using a pastry brush, generously coat each wrapped sausage with glaze. Be sure to use all of it!

6 Bake for 11-12 minutes or until dough is golden brown and Lit'l Smokies are warmed through.

7 Allow pigs in a blanket to cool for 5 minutes.

8 Serve as desired.

ingredients

8 ounces crescent roll dough

24 Lit'l Smokies, or similar type of pre-cooked sausages or hot dogs

4 tablespoons unsalted butter, melted

3/4 teaspoon dried minced onion

1/2 teaspoon Dijon mustard

1/2 teaspoon poppy seeds

1/2 teaspoon sesame seeds

1/2 teaspoon Worcestershire sauce

1/4 teaspoon garlic powder

ingredients

1 pound blue crab meat, drained and any shells/cartilage removed

20 saltine crackers, finely crushed

1 tablespoon chopped fresh chives, or parsley, plus more for garnish

1/4 cup mayonnaise

1 large egg

1 tablespoon Dijon mustard

1 teaspoon Old Bay seasoning

1 tablespoon Worcestershire sauce

1/4 cup canola oil

1 tablespoon salted butter, cut into 6 pieces

chesapeake bay crab cakes

Indulge in homemade crab cakes with succulent blue crab meat and minimal filler. A classic dish with irresistible flavor and a perfect blend of seasonings.

makes: 6 servings   **prep**: 20 mins   **chill**: 3 hours   **cook**: 16 mins

directions

1 In a large bowl, add crab meat, crushed saltine crackers, and chives, then gently fold together until mixed, being careful not to break up crab meat.

2 In a separate bowl, whisk together mayonnaise, egg, Dijon mustard, Old Bay seasoning, and Worcestershire sauce.

3 Pour sauce over crab mixture, then use a spatula gently fold ingredients together until incorporated.

4 Cover bowl with plastic wrap and chill crab cake mix in refrigerator for 3 hours.

5 When ready to cook, preheat oven to broil on high. Make sure there's a rack placed 6-8 inches from top of oven.

6 In a 10-inch cast iron skillet (or other oven-safe skillet), add canola oil and warm over medium heat.

7 While skillet heats up, remove crab cake mix from refrigerator. Gently mix crab meat a final time, then scoop out and form 6 large crab cakes.

8 Add crab cakes to skillet and cook until underside of crab cakes are golden brown, about 5-8 minutes. Make sure to check each under each crab cake every minute or so to ensure none are cooking too fast.

9 Remove pan from heat. Add a piece of sliced butter on top of each crab cake, then place pan in heated oven on top rack.

10 1 tablespoon salted butter

11 Broil crab cakes for 6-8 minutes or until tops are browned to desired level. Keep a close eye on them; crab cakes can burn quickly.

12 Allow crab cakes to rest for 5 minutes.

13 Serve as desired.

jalapeno popper pinwheels

Made with a blend of creamy cheese, crispy bacon, and spicy jalapeno, these pinwheels deliver an unforgettable flavor with a kick of spice.

makes: 45 servings **prep**: 20 mins
chill: 4 hours

ingredients

8 ounces cream cheese, softened

1/3 cup sour cream

1 1/2 cups shredded sharp cheddar cheese

1/3 cup pre-cooked bacon bits

1/4 cup chopped jalapeno pepper, seeds and ribs removed

2 stalks green onion, thinly sliced

5 8-inch flour tortillas

directions

1 Using a stand mixer (or hand mixer + medium bowl), whip together cream cheese and sour cream on medium-high speed until smooth, about 3-5 minutes.

2 Remove bowl from mixer. Add cheese, bacon, jalapeno, and green onion to bowl. Use a spatula to gently fold them into cream cheese mixture.

3 On a clean work surface, lay a tortilla. Take 1/5th of cream cheese mixture and spread it evenly across tortilla, leaving a 1/2 inch border. Tightly roll tortilla to form a log. Repeat this step for remaining 4 tortillas.

4 Wrap tortilla logs tightly with plastic wrap, folding the ends of plastic wrap underneath to secure. Place wrapped tortillas in refrigerator for at least 4 hours or ideally overnight.

5 When ready to serve, bring wrapped tortillas out and remove plastic wrap. Cut into 1/2 inch slices, creating roughly 9 or 10 pinwheels per tortilla.

6 Serve as desired.

ingredients

8 ounces cream cheese, softened

2/3 cup ketchup

1 tablespoon horseradish, or to taste

8 ounces cooked salad shrimp, chopped and divided

chopped fresh parsley, for garnish (optional)

cream cheese shrimp dip

This 1960s-inspired cream cheese shrimp dip has all the best qualities of a retro appetizer: smooth cream cheese, tangy flavors, and tender salad shrimp.

makes: 6 servings   **prep**: 15 mins

directions

1 Place cream cheese (still as a block) on a serving platter, then set aside.

2 In a small bowl, whisk together ketchup and horseradish until combined.

3 Add half of salad shrimp to bowl, then toss to coat with sauce.

4 Pour sauced shrimp over cream cheese, then top with remaining salad shrimp. Garnish with chopped fresh parsley (optional).

5 Serve as desired.

dirty martini dip

With a creamy base flavored briny olives, savory spices, and sharp blue cheese, this dirty martini party dip is just as fun to eat as the cocktail is to drink.

makes: 6 servings   **prep**: 20 mins

directions

1. Using a stand mixer (or a hand mixer + large bowl), mix together cream cheese, sour cream, mayonnaise, olive juice, garlic powder, onion powder, salt, and pepper on medium-high speed until smooth, about 2-4 minutes.

2. Remove bowl from mixer. Add chopped olives and blue cheese to bowl. Use a spatula to gently fold all ingredients together.

3. Transfer dip to a serving bowl and garnish with more olives, blue cheese, and chives as garnish (all optional).

4. Serve as desired.

ingredients

8 ounces cream cheese, softened

3/4 cup sour cream

1/4 cup mayonnaise

1 tablespoon olive juice, from the jar of olives

1/2 teaspoon garlic powder

1/2 teaspoon onion powder

1/4 teaspoon kosher salt

1/2 teaspoon black pepper

3/4 cup pimento-stuffed olives, chopped, plus more for garnish (optional)

1/2 cup crumbled blue cheese, plus more for garnish (optional)

1 tablespoon chopped fresh chives, for garnish (optional)

ingredients

5 1/2 cups water, divided

2 1/4 teaspoons active dry yeast

1 tablespoon light brown sugar

3 1/4 cups all-purpose flour, plus more for consistency and kneading

4 tablespoons salted butter, melted, divided

2 teaspoons salt

1/4 cup baking soda

2 tablespoons coarse sea salt, for garnish

soft pretzels

With the perfect balance of a soft and chewy texture these soft pretzels are made with a simple yeast dough and infused with classic buttery flavor.

makes: 8 servings   **prep**: 2 hours   **cook**: 40 minutes

directions

1 In a microwave-safe bowl, add 1 1/2 cups water. Heat in microwave at 15-second intervals until it reaches 115-120°F. Do not exceed 120°F.

2 Mix yeast and brown sugar into bowl. Let it bloom for 5 minutes.

3 In a stand mixer with dough hook (or by hand in a large bowl), combine flour, 2 tablespoons melted butter, salt, and yeast mixture. Knead on low for 8-10 minutes (or 10-15 minutes by hand) until dough is slightly sticky and rebounds when poked. If necessary, incorporate more flour for consistency, 1/4 cup at a time, up to an extra 1/2 cup.

4 Spray another mixing bowl with cooking spray. Transfer dough to bowl, rolling to coat with spray. Cover with plastic wrap and let dough rise in a warm, dry area for 60-90 minutes.

5 When ready to form pretzels, preheat oven to 350°F. Line a baking sheet with parchment paper. Dust a clean work area with flour. Bring out bowl with dough and remove plastic wrap. Firmly punch dough down, releasing any air.

6 Divide dough into 8 pieces, roll each into a 25-30 inch rope. Shape each rope into a U, with curve facing away. Cross and twist ends, then fold them back, pressing into bottom of U shape. Resulting pretzel should look like a rounded heart with a twist in center. Place pretzels on baking sheet.

7 Boil 4 cups water with baking soda in a large saucepan until dissolved. Working in batches of 1-2, boil pretzels for 20-30 seconds, then use a slotted spatula to transfer them back to baking sheet.

8 Sprinkle boiled pretzels with coarse sea salt.

9 Bake pretzels for 16-20 minutes or until golden.

10 Brush with 2 tablespoons melted butter, then let cool on a wire cooling rack for 5-10 minutes.

11 Serve as desired.

ingredients

1 tablespoon salted butter

1/4 cup finely chopped white onion

2 teaspoons minced fresh garlic

1 tablespoon all-purpose flour

2 1/2 cups shredded cheddar cheese

13 ounces evaporated milk

1 cup diced tomato, plus more for garnish

4 ounces fire roasted green chiles, chopped (more or less to taste)

2 tablespoons milk

1 pinch salt, to taste

1 pinch black pepper, to taste

queso dip

Ultra creamy and cheesy, this easy queso dip tastes just like what they serve at restaurants. Perfect snack food for parties or quiet nights on the couch.

makes: 6 servings **prep**: 10 mins
cook: 25 mins

directions

1 In a saucepan over medium heat, melt butter. Add onion and garlic to saucepan and cook, stirring occasionally, until garlic is fragrant and onion is translucent, about 2-4 minutes.

2 Sprinkle flour over cooked onion and garlic. Cook, stirring constantly, for 1-2 minutes or until flour is fully incorporated but not browned.

3 Add cheese, evaporated milk, tomato, chiles, milk, and salt and pepper (to taste) to saucepan. Stir and cook sauce until cheese is completely melted and creamy. Taste test dip and season with more salt or pepper, if needed. If sauce seems too thick, another 1-2 tablespoons of milk until desired consistency is reached.

4 Transfer dip to a serving bowl and garnish with more tomatoes (optional).

5 Serve as desired.

hot pimento cheese dip

A melted blend of savory cheeses, a few spices, and sliced pimentos make this Kentucky Derby appetizer a crowd-pleasing favorite.

makes: 6 servings   **prep**: 10 mins
cook: 20 mins

directions

1 Preheat oven to 375°F. Spray a shallow baking dish with cooking spray, then set aside.

2 Using a stand mixer (or a hand mixer + large bowl), whip mayonnaise, cream cheese, Worcestershire sauce, hot sauce, ground mustard, salt, and pepper on medium-high speed until mostly smooth, about 3-5 minutes.

3 Remove bowl from mixer and add cheddar cheese, Pepper Jack cheese, pimentos, and green onion to bowl. Use a spatula to gently fold all ingredients together until thoroughly mixed.

4 Pour cheese mixture into prepared baking dish and gently smooth out top so that it's flat.

5 Bake dip for 15-20 minutes or until cheese is melted and bubbly.

6 Serve as desired.

ingredients

1 cup mayonnaise

8 ounces cream cheese, softened

1 teaspoon Worcestershire sauce

1 teaspoon hot sauce

1/2 teaspoon ground mustard

1 pinch salt, to taste

1 pinch black pepper, to taste

2 cups shredded cheddar cheese

2 cups shredded Pepper Jack cheese

1/2 cup sliced pimentos, drained

1/2 cup chopped green onion

dippers and sides

When it comes to serving dips and finger foods, you can never go wrong with adding a few accompanyments and dipping options to your serving platter.

Feel free to chose any (or many) from the following list to fill out your spread:

Ritz Crackers: Buttery and slightly salty, ideal for cheese dips and creamy textures.

Tortilla Chips or Scoops: Corn-based and crunchy, perfect for chunky dips like guacamole, salsa, and queso.

Pretzels or Pretzel Rods: Salty and malty, best for tangy, creamy, and spicy dips.

Toasted Bread: Crunchy with a toasted flavor, excellent for absorbing flavors.

Saltine Crackers: Mild and slightly salty, complementing seafood dips and various creamy dips without overpowering them.

Vegetable Sticks: Fresh and crunchy, offering a healthy contrast to rich, creamy dips like ranch or blue cheese.

Pita Chips: Earthy and toasted, sturdy enough for thick dips like hummus and tzatziki.

Rice Crackers: Light and airy, ideal for lighter dips such as ceviche or ahi poke, and a good gluten-free option.

Naan or Bagel Pieces: Soft and pillowy, these great for scooping heavy, saucy dips.

Bagel Chips or Melba Toast: Very crunchy and toasted, holds up well under strong flavored dips like garlic or roasted red pepper.

thank you

Thank you so much for picking up my cookbook—I hope you'll love whipping up these recipes as much as I enjoyed creating them! And if you're craving even more easy entertaining eats, be sure to pop over to my website (or follow me on social media) for additional tips, regular updates, and new recipes to try.

Just scan the QR code below and you'll be on your way!

Facebook: facebook.com/homemadehooplah
Instagram: instagram.com/homemadehooplah
Twitter: twitter.com/homemadehooplah
Pinterest: pinterest.com/homemadehooplah/

happy cooking!

flavor index

flavor index